EVERY KID'S GUIDE TO GOALS

How to Choose, Set, and Achieve Goals That Matter to You.

Karleen Tauszik

Text and layout copyright 2017 by Karleen Tauszik.
Cover illustrations from iStockPhoto.com, contributor FatCamera, and BigstockPhoto.com, contributor RawPixel.com.
Cover design copyright 2017 by Karleen Tauszik.

All rights reserved, including the right of reproduction in whole or in part in any form. The final Goal Worksheet may be photocopied for personal use.

Summary: This book guides children on how to choose goals, how to set them, and how to achieve them, giving kids a valuable skill that will benefit them throughout life.

ISBN: 978-0-9904899-5-5

Karleen Tauszik is the author of books for children, primarily in the 8 to 12-year-old age range. She has worked in Human Resources for over 15 years and she's passionate about helping people find success in their lives. Visit her on the web at KarleenT.com, where you can see her other books for kids and sign up for her newsletter.

This book belongs to

_____
(my name)

It was given to me by

_____

on _____ when I was
    (date with year)

_____ years old.

*But all the magic I have known,
I've had to make myself.*

--Shel Silverstein,
Where the Sidewalk Ends

Do you dream of something you'd like to do or have, but you don't know how to get started? Do you wish you could get a better grade in math or stop fighting with your little brother or sister, but you're not sure how to make those things happen? Do you think setting goals can only be done at the beginning of the year, with all the people who make New Year's resolutions?

If so, this book is for you.

You'll learn the difference between a wish, a dream, and a goal.

You'll learn about how to make sure your goals are SMART, so you can actually achieve them. (The letters S-M-A-R-T stand for special keys to goal success. Keep reading to find out what they are.)

You'll also learn how to set goals, stick with them and achieve what you want.

All you need is a pen or pencil, some creative thinking, and a target or deadline. With this book, you'll be able to work toward things that are important to you and achieve the goals you set.

Let's get started!

Why set goals?

Why should you set goals? Isn't that something that's just for adults?

You've probably seen plenty of grown-ups make big resolutions at New Years, and by Valentine's Day, they've forgotten all about them. In fact, 95% of the people who make New Year's resolutions give up (if they ever got started) by the end of January.

So why should you bother?

The main reason to set goals is that you want to improve something in your life. Sure, you can float along through life and not care. You can ignore or put up with the things that frustrate you. You can be satisfied with how you perform in school or in your extra-curricular activities. In other words, you can settle for what life gives you. Or you can take steps to improve your life.

It's <u>your</u> choice.

The second reason to set a goal is to be able to measure how you're doing and know when you have achieved what you want. Good goals have a deadline and they usually have another measurement attached to them, like an amount you'd like to save up or a grade or score you'd like to achieve.

For example, you might set a goal to save up ten dollars by the weekend before Mother's Day so you can get Mom a nice present. You have a concrete date and dollar amount you are shooting for. But if you said, "It would be great to have more money so someday I could buy Mom a nice present," that's a wish. It doesn't have a measurement and deadline to tell you if you were successful. It's not a goal.

The third and best reason to try goal setting is that it will cause you to think, take action, and work toward something that's important to you. When you achieve your goal, or even if you come close, it will give you the confidence to shoot for the next goal on your list.

Your parents and teachers have probably told you that you have great potential. Actually, it's not just you—everyone has great potential. Everyone is capable of becoming better in areas of their life. But most people don't bother. In fact, less than 3% of all Americans have written goals. The average person is…well…average, happy to float through life without achieving much of anything.

That doesn't need to be you. When you learn how to set goals and achieve them, you'll be able to use more of your potential, rising you above the average crowd. That can benefit you for the rest of your life.

Your Dream List

What would you like to improve or change in your life? Think about things you want to do, how you want to be, and things you'd like to have. Consider the different areas of your life: school, extra-curricular activities, health, friendships, family, money, something you want to save up for, the way you spend your time, things you want to learn about and so on. Daydream for a bit, then list all of the items you think of here:

_____

_____

_____

_____

_____

_____

_____

Don't worry—you can always come back to this page to add more ideas. And I've given you more space for your list on the next page.

Dream List Review

Now that you've made your dream list, let's review it.

Are there things on your list that you can't control? Mark them with an X. For example, if you wrote something like, "I want Grandpa to come home from the hospital and not be sick," that's something you can't control. You CAN call him every day or make him a Get Well Soon card. Both of those things have the potential to make his time in the hospital a bit more pleasant. But you can't control his illness or how long he stays in the hospital.

Now look over your list and mark the top thing you'd like to work on. Don't pick something too easy, but also don't pick something too difficult. Let's start with a medium sized dream and see if we can turn it into an achievable goal.

The top thing I'd like to work on first is _____

_____

_____

But What's a Goal?

You've made your dream list. But how can you change those dreams into goals? First, let's figure out what a goal is.

Have you ever had someone tell you something they wanted to happen, and you thought, "You wish!" or "Dream on!" You had a strong feeling that the person wouldn't achieve what he or she said. Why did you feel that way? Did their dream seem to be too big? Unrealistic? Too far off into the future?

Let's look at the differences between wishing, dreaming, and setting a goal. Here is the meaning of each one.

Wish: to want, desire, or long for.

Dream: to think or conceive of something in a very remote way. To imagine as if in a dream.

Goal: the result or achievement toward which effort is directed. The aim or the end.

Do you see the difference?

Let's look at an example.

You can say, "I **wish** my little sister didn't follow me around and bug me so much when I get home from school. It's so frustrating. And then I get in trouble with Dad when I lose my patience."

Or, "I **dream** about the day when my little sister goes to school. When she has more friends, maybe she won't bug me so much when I get home. I can't wait!"

Or how about, "My **goal** is to spend the first half hour after I get home with my little sister. If I have my snack with her and play and talk with her for that time, she'll more likely leave me alone so I can do my homework before dinner."

Do you see the difference now? It's ACTION.

You can wish and dream all you want, but it won't change the situation. Action is the key that will unlock the door to your goal. In the next sections, you'll learn how to make a plan of action that will work for YOU.

Smart Goals

Remember in the introduction how I mentioned SMART goals? Here's where you'll learn about what each letter means.

Specific – what exactly do I want to achieve?
Measurable – how will I track my progress? How much, by when?
Attainable – Is this goal realistic for me? Do I have what I need to attain it? If not, how can I get what I need?
Relevant – Why does this matter to me? Why do I want to do this?
Time-oriented – When will I complete this goal? What's my deadline?

Go back to your dream list review on page 7. Read over the top goal you wrote at the bottom of that page and make sure you can answer all five of the S-M-A-R-T requirements. If not, either adjust that goal or pick another goal from the dream list. Make sure you have a SMART goal.

Next, you'll fill in your Goal Worksheet on the next two pages. Did you know that writing out your goal increases your chances of achieving it? Yes, people who write their goals are about 40% more likely to achieve them than people who just think about their goals. That's why you should use the Goal Worksheet (or at least a notebook) anytime you set a goal.

Today's Date _____

My Goal Worksheet

My goal is _____

_____

_____

My goal is SMART.

☐ It's <u>S</u>pecific. I know exactly what I want.

☐ It's <u>M</u>easurable. I know how much I want to do.

☐ It's <u>A</u>chievable. I can do this. If I need help, I can ask _____

☐ It's <u>R</u>elevant. This matters to me because _____

_____

☐ It's <u>T</u>ime-Oriented. My deadline for this goal is _____

Are there any obstacles in my way? If so, how can I deal with them?

_____

Do I need any special skills or knowledge to achieve this? _____

_____

Is there anyone I need to work with? _____

Who can help to keep me on track? _____

If I achieve this goal, my benefits will be _____

_____

To get started, I need to _____

_____

_____

_____

The steps I need to take to complete this goal are:

Review

Did you achieve your goal? If so, congratulations!

If not, did you come close? What kept you from hitting the goal? Was it in your control or out of your control? Did you need reminders? What did you learn?

Even the best goal setters don't reach every goal they set. Remember, even if you came close, you're now further ahead than you were before you set the goal. Try again.

Go back to your dream list. Review it.

Do you want to add anything?

Do you want to cross off some items that you no longer care about?

Move on to your next goal or two. There are five more goal worksheets in this book, plus one reserved for photocopying. I hope you are able to achieve many of the goals you have in mind for your life!

Today's Date _____

My Goal Worksheet

My goal is _____

_____

_____

My goal is SMART.

☐ It's <u>S</u>pecific. I know exactly what I want.

☐ It's <u>M</u>easurable. I know how much I want to do.

☐ It's <u>A</u>chievable. I can do this. If I need help, I can ask _____

☐ It's <u>R</u>elevant. This matters to me because _____

_____

☐ It's <u>T</u>ime-Oriented. My deadline for this goal is _____

Are there any obstacles in my way? If so, how can I deal with them?

_____

Do I need any special skills or knowledge to achieve this? _____

_____

Is there anyone I need to work with? _____

Who can help to keep me on track? _____

If I achieve this goal, my benefits will be _____

_____

To get started, I need to _____

_____

_____

_____

The steps I need to take to complete this goal are:

Today's Date _____

My Goal Worksheet

My goal is _____

_____

_____

My goal is SMART.

☐ It's <u>S</u>pecific. I know exactly what I want.

☐ It's <u>M</u>easurable. I know how much I want to do.

☐ It's <u>A</u>chievable. I can do this. If I need help, I can ask _____

☐ It's <u>R</u>elevant. This matters to me because _____

_____

☐ It's <u>T</u>ime-Oriented. My deadline for this goal is _____

Are there any obstacles in my way? If so, how can I deal with them?

_____

Do I need any special skills or knowledge to achieve this? _____

_____

Is there anyone I need to work with? _____

Who can help to keep me on track? _____

If I achieve this goal, my benefits will be _____

_____

To get started, I need to _____

_____

_____

_____

The steps I need to take to complete this goal are:

Today's Date _____

My Goal Worksheet

My goal is _____

_____

_____

My goal is SMART.

☐ It's Specific. I know exactly what I want.

☐ It's Measurable. I know how much I want to do.

☐ It's Achievable. I can do this. If I need help, I can ask _____

☐ It's Relevant. This matters to me because _____

_____

☐ It's Time-Oriented. My deadline for this goal is _____

Are there any obstacles in my way? If so, how can I deal with them?

_____

Do I need any special skills or knowledge to achieve this? _____

_____

Is there anyone I need to work with? _____

Who can help to keep me on track? _____

If I achieve this goal, my benefits will be _____

_____

To get started, I need to _____

_____

_____

_____

The steps I need to take to complete this goal are:

_____

_____

_____

_____

_____

_____

_____

_____

_____

_____

_____

_____

_____

Today's Date _____

My Goal Worksheet

My goal is _____

_____

_____

My goal is SMART.

☐ It's <u>S</u>pecific. I know exactly what I want.

☐ It's <u>M</u>easurable. I know how much I want to do.

☐ It's <u>A</u>chievable. I can do this. If I need help, I can ask _____

☐ It's <u>R</u>elevant. This matters to me because _____

_____

☐ It's <u>T</u>ime-Oriented. My deadline for this goal is _____

Are there any obstacles in my way? If so, how can I deal with them?

_____

Do I need any special skills or knowledge to achieve this? _____

_____

Is there anyone I need to work with? _____

Who can help to keep me on track? _____

If I achieve this goal, my benefits will be _____

_____

To get started, I need to _____

_____

_____

_____

The steps I need to take to complete this goal are:

_____

_____

_____

_____

_____

_____

_____

_____

_____

_____

_____

Today's Date _____

My Goal Worksheet

My goal is _____

_____

_____

My goal is SMART.

☐ It's <u>S</u>pecific. I know exactly what I want.

☐ It's <u>M</u>easurable. I know how much I want to do.

☐ It's <u>A</u>chievable. I can do this. If I need help, I can ask _____

☐ It's <u>R</u>elevant. This matters to me because _____

_____

☐ It's <u>T</u>ime-Oriented. My deadline for this goal is _____

Are there any obstacles in my way? If so, how can I deal with them?

_____

Do I need any special skills or knowledge to achieve this? _____

_____

Is there anyone I need to work with? _____

Who can help to keep me on track? _____

If I achieve this goal, my benefits will be _____

_____

To get started, I need to _____

_____

_____

_____

The steps I need to take to complete this goal are:

Congratulations!
You've used up all six of your
Goal Worksheets!
There's one more after this page.
Use it to make as many
photocopies as you need
to continue your goal-setting
adventures.

Today's Date _____

My Goal Worksheet

My goal is _____

_____

_____

My goal is SMART.

☐ It's <u>S</u>pecific. I know exactly what I want.

☐ It's <u>M</u>easurable. I know how much I want to do.

☐ It's <u>A</u>chievable. I can do this. If I need help, I can ask _____

☐ It's <u>R</u>elevant. This matters to me because _____

_____

☐ It's <u>T</u>ime-Oriented. My deadline for this goal is _____

Are there any obstacles in my way? If so, how can I deal with them?

_____

Do I need any special skills or knowledge to achieve this? _____

_____

Is there anyone I need to work with? _____

Who can help to keep me on track? _____

If I achieve this goal, my benefits will be _____

_____

To get started, I need to _____

_____

_____

_____

The steps I need to take to complete this goal are:

About the Author

Karleen Tauszik writes books mostly for children ages 8 to 12. Her goal as an author is to get kids to LOVE reading. As a child, Karleen had the goal (not met) to read every book in the children's section of her local library. Through the books she writes, she hopes to instill that kind of fervor for reading in kids today.

Karleen is also passionate about success, people's careers, and goal setting. That's why she wrote this book. She's also the author of *When I Grow Up, I Want To Be...*, an annual career possibility journal for kids. It's been listed as one of "2017's Most Popular New Toys for Kids This Christmas."

Karleen is married to a professional ventriloquist and magician, and they live in the Tampa Bay area. Learn more about Karleen at her website, KarleenT.com.

www.ingramcontent.com/pod-product-compliance
Lightning Source LLC
Chambersburg PA
CBHW080519020526
44113CB00055B/2535